N 6512.5 .A7 W428 1992
26001260
American art deco

S0-ARL-613

N 6512.5 .A7 W428 1992
26001260
American art deco

Stockton University
Library
Galloway, NJ 08205

AMERICAN ART DECO

Stockton University
Library
Galloway, NJ 08205

AMERICAN ART DECO

Eva Weber

Crescent Books
New York

Stockton University
Library
Galloway, NJ 08205

Copyright © 1992 Brompton Books Corp.

All rights reserved. No part of this publication
may be reproduced, stored in a retrieval system or
transmitted in any form by any means, electronic,
mechanical, photocopying or otherwise, without
first obtaining the written permission of the copyright
owner.

This 1992 edition published by Crescent Books,
distributed by Outlet Book Company, Inc.,
a Random House Company,
225 Park Avenue South
New York, New York 10003

Produced by
Brompton Books Corporation
15 Sherwood Place
Greenwich, CT 06830

ISBN 0-517-06712-9

8 7 6 5 4 3 2 1

Printed and bound in Hong Kong

Page 1: **Frederick Carder**
Grille panel, ca. early 1930s
colorless lead glass press
Gift of the Corning Glass Works
The Corning Museum of Glass
Corning, NY

Page 2: **William Van Alen**
Chrysler Building, 1930
New York, NY
Photo: Peter Mauss/ESTO

Pages 4-5: **Frederick Carder**
Grille panel, ca. 1930s
green glass pressed
Gift of Corning Glass Works
The Corning Museum of Glass
Corning, NY

Contents

INTRODUCTION

During the 1920s and 1930s art deco flourished as a truly international style, influencing modernist designers in many areas: interiors, furniture, textiles, ceramics, glassware, metalware, a wide range of household accessories, as well as architecture. Although examples of art deco design preceded the 1925 Paris *Exposition Internationale des Arts Décoratifs et Industriels Modernes*, which gave the style its name, it was this event that publicized the style, made it fashionable, and established the preeminence of French designers in the production of luxury furniture and opulent ornamental objects.

The art deco style, which traveled to the United States and other countries, drew on a wide variety of historical and contemporary sources. Then recent archaeological discoveries in the Mediterranean region and in the pre-Columbian Americas provided the style with motifs and techniques from the Minoan, archaic Greek, Assyrian, and ancient Egyptian civilizations, as well as from the Mayan and Aztec cultures of Mexico and Central America. Important too were the recurrent classical revival styles, with their subtext of Greek and Roman mythology. At the same time anthropological investigations, along with the commercial inroads of colonial expansionism, brought to western attention the decorative traditions of Africans, Native Americans, and the cultures of Southeast Asia and the South Pacific.

Just as central to the art deco style were the avant-garde art movements of the early twentieth century. From cubism came stylization and geometric abstraction, while the vibrant colors of art deco were shared with fauvism, Orphism, and synchronism. Art deco shared with futurism and vorticism a fascination with dynamic movement, which was expressed by means of diagonal ray lines and zigzags, as well as the imagery of machine technology and of the modern city – an imagery also explored by the American precisionists. And, like constructivism, art deco experimented with innovative combinations of industrial materials with an emphasis on mass production and on a collaborative attempt to create an aesthetically unified environment that would be responsive to modern needs. It is in this respect that art deco's underlying spirit was utopian or propagandistic.

And, finally, art deco adapted elements from the decorative arts styles that immediately preceded it. From the arts and crafts movements in England and the United States came some

Left: Louis Boileau's highly ornamented design for the Pomone Pavilion at the 1925 Paris exposition is a fine example of French art deco.

Right: The Pyramid of the Sun from the Teotihuacan culture of ancient America.

of its collaborative spirit, utopian fervor, and the idea of the aesthetically unified environment. After the turn of the century, art nouveau increasingly came to be seen as decadent, but it had forged the way for art deco. Art nouveau had been a deliberate attempt to establish an entirely new style, free of all historicist motifs and associations with the past. As the decorative equivalent of the symbolist movement in art and literature, French art nouveau was marked by the use of sinuous, elongated, stylized plants, and other forms derived from nature. As its immediate ancestor, art nouveau lent to art deco its floral and faunal imagery, which was transformed from its voluptuous curvilinear asymmetry into the sharp-edged, syncopated geometry of art deco. More closely related to art deco was the elegantly rectilinear variant of art nouveau developed by Charles Rennie MacIntosh in Glasgow, by the Munich secessionists of the *Jugendstil* in Germany, and by Josef Hoffmann and other practitioners of the *Sezessionstil* in Vienna. Indeed, Hoffmann's Brussels masterpiece, the *Palais Stoclet*, was an important antecedent of art deco architecture. Hoffmann designed not only the building but the luxurious, visually unified furniture and accessories. By 1910, Hoffmann was making stepped, or ziggurat-shaped case furniture that was, perhaps, more art deco than anything else.

An essential component of art deco was its interpretation of the times in which it existed. The fashionable, artistic, social, political, and technological events of the age were incorporated into the imagery of art deco. Thus the colorful exotic costumes and sets by Leon Bakst for the 1909 Paris performances of Sergei Diaghilev's Ballets Russes fired the imagination of French designers. The glamorous world of the roaring twenties – with its jazz music, Charleston and other lively dances, fashionable nightclubs, cocktail culture, liberated flappers, and cabaret and vaudeville performers – was a fertile source of motifs for designers in Europe and America. The technological marvels of the age – automobiles, airplanes, ocean liners, trains, bridges, factories, grain elevators, and skyscrapers – also were celebrated endlessly in art deco design. A cross-fertilization also existed between art deco and the cinema. The skyscraper and the futuristic aerodynamic curves of the streamline phase of art deco had much in common with the scenic design of science fiction films. Theatrical revues and movie musicals also drew on art deco ideas and motifs. And when the party came to an end with the 1929 stock market crash, art deco accordingly downshifted into a more somber and conservative vein, now praising heroic workers in the classical mode and exploring traditional and nationalist values in didactic murals influenced by Diego Rivera.

Just as the imagery of art deco changed to suit the times, so

7

did the style itself change from the 1920s to the 1930s. This evolution was more apparent in the United States, where the art deco style arrived later and persisted longer than elsewhere. Historians of design generally agree that the designation "art deco" encompasses three distinct but related design trends. A conservative variant of art deco architecture known as "classical moderne" was built throughout the art deco decades, although it came to the forefront during the depression years of the 1930s. In contrast to the more flamboyant manifestations of art deco, this was a restrained architecture, blending a simplified modernistic neoclassicism with an austere form of geometric and stylized relief sculpture, murals and other ornament, on both the exterior and interior.

The most distinctive form of art deco architecture was what is now referred to as "zigzag moderne" – the exotically dynamic style of such skyscrapers as the Chrysler and Empire State buildings. The description "zigzag" refers to the geometric and repetitive stylized ornament of zigzags, angular patterns, abstract animal and plant motifs, sunbursts, astrological symbolism, frozen fountains and related motifs that were applied richly in metalwork, mosaic, etched glass, sculptural relief, and mural

form to the exterior and interior of the buildings, many of which were ziggurat-shaped.

The third major expression of art deco was the 1930s "streamline moderne" style – a sleek aerodynamic style of rounded corners and horizontal parallel bands known as speed stripes. It was a style developed and enthusiastically promoted by such industrial designers as Norman Bel Geddes and Raymond Loewy, who used it in the redesign of transport vehicles and household appliances. In architecture, the style often included porthole windows, extensive use of glass block and flat roof tops.

There were several regional variants of the art deco style in the United States. Southern California's style was inspired by the ancient buildings of the Maya and Aztec. The most important buildings of Aztec deco were designed by Frank Lloyd Wright, using geometrically patterned textile blocks and poured concrete in stepped-back massive contours. Another regional variant, Pueblo deco – based on a fusion of Pueblo Indian, Spanish colonial, and California mission revival architecture – developed in west Texas, New Mexico, and Arizona. Derived from the area's vernacular white adobe buildings, it

Left: Josef Hoffmann's Palais Stoclet in Brussels, 1905-11: the first major Wiener Werkstätte commission.

Right: Sunflower Jardiniere, 1925-30, Roseville Pottery.

Below: Film director Fritz Lang was inspired by the New York City skyline to create the masterpiece of art deco set design *Metropolis*, 1926.

Left: National Farmers' Bank in Owatonna, Minnesota, was Louis Sullivan's last major architectural statement.

was essentially a style of massive forms, flat-topped arches and primitive columns, with ornament based on symbolic and ceremonial Navaho, Hopi, and Pueblo Indian motifs from pottery, basketwork, jewelry, and textiles. Other motifs included cacti, cowboys, and sun symbols.

Perhaps the best known of the regional variants is the tropical deco of Florida. Usually tropical deco buildings were constructed inexpensively of stuccoed concrete. Here the aerodynamic curves of the streamline style were accompanied by zigzag style setbacks, polychromy, and stylized organic and abstract ornament. The resort hotels, apartment buildings, and houses in the style were often white, or more frequently were painted with such sensuous pastel hues as flamingo pink, sea green, and banana yellow. Sometimes the facades sported the machine-age masts previously seen on zigzag style skyscrapers. Tropical deco's unique features included cantilevered sunshades over windows, octagonal and porthole windows, flagstaff parapets, and deck-like balconies. The regional marine imagery included such motifs as dolphins, herons, mermaids, seashells, alligators, tropical vegetation, flamingos, sunrises, fountains, palm trees, and stylized waves and clouds.

Visual richness was a prevalent feature of art deco architecture in America, reflecting in part the nation's wealth and optimism in the 1920s. Comparatively speaking, the Europeans, apart from their experimental exposition buildings, built a smaller stock of art deco buildings and in general these were of a conservative nature, usually adhering to the classical moderne style. The English described their relatively few flamboyant art deco buildings – an example was the Hoover Factory – as being in the "America style."

The picturesqueness of American art deco architecture had deep roots in the past. Louis Sullivan, who is considered one of the few American practitioners of art nouveau, used patterned floral ornament in cast iron and colorful terra cotta to emphasize the different parts of a building. His use of vertical piers alternating with recessed ornamented spandrels later became an essential feature of art deco design. Alone among the white Beaux Arts buildings at the 1893 Chicago Exposition, Sulli-

van's exotically decorated orientalist Transportation Building looked ahead to the 1920s. The theories, writings, and buildings of Sullivan had a profound impact on the development of American architecture, the skyscraper, and on the use of architectural ornament.

The modernist ideas of Finland's Eliel Saarinen, whose second prize in the 1922 Chicago Tribune Tower competition was to bring him to the United States, inspired American architect Bertram Goodhue to design, beginning in 1916, the Nebraska State Capitol. This building, which reflects a familiarity with Saarinen's Helsinki Railroad Station, fundamentally established the prototype for civic and public construction in the classical moderne style. The capitol building was an innovative amalgam of modernistic and classical, of skyscraper and temple, with a stable simplified mass, an arched, sculpturally ornamented entrance, and a dramatic soaring golden-domed tower. Inside, the work on the illustrative murals, mosaics and friezes adorning the ceremonial chambers took some forty years to complete.

The widespread use of opulently stylish interiors, even within the context of such restrained classical moderne buildings such as banks, was common to American art deco during the zigzag era of the 1920s and extended as well to the depression years of the 1930s. Some of the most extravagant interiors were those assembled for movie theaters, hotels, restaurants, and nightclubs. Ocean liners, trains, shops, and even the private offices and residences of the fashionably inclined and economically able also were transformed by the aura of zigzag style luxury, or later by the sleek purity of the streamline style. Among the ranks of the interior designers were not only the leading art deco architects and furniture makers, but also the graphic and theatrical designers who later were to form the core of the industrial design movement of the 1930s.

While in France the graphic and illustrative arts played a central role in the expression and dissemination of the art deco style, in the United States their influence was secondary. Certainly, an architectural illustrator of the stature of Hugh Ferriss was important in publicizing and promoting the skyscraper style by means of his romantically abstracted and visionary renderings of art deco buildings. The bold stylized black-and-white book illustrations by the prolific Rockwell Kent, Lynd Ward, and John Vassos were quintessentially art deco, but limited in distribution. A far wider audience was reached by such fashionable magazines as *Vogue, Harper's Bazaar,* and *Vanity Fair* who commissioned covers and illustrations by leading French illustrators and graphic artists such as Cassandre, Carlu, and Erté, as well as by Americans.

The magazines also employed such leading photographers as Edward Steichen and Margaret Bourke White, and their stylish art deco photographs constituted a uniquely American contribution to this medium. The art deco photographs were characterized by the use of dynamically oblique or diagonal camera angles, dramatic close-ups, strong contrasts of light and shadow, and silhouetting and mirroring effects, emphasizing rhythmic repetition of elements, and exploiting flattened geometric patterns. In photography and the graphic arts, as well as in the area of furnishings and interior design, art deco possessed a particular appeal for the commercial client.

During the later 1920s and 1930s, international expositions provided a major showcase for art deco design and architecture. Although the expositions were primarily vehicles of nationalism and commercialism, the fairs also stimulated experimentation in the arts and design. Most leading architects, artists, and designers – many of them central to art deco – were involved in the planning and execution of projects for these extravaganzas. Smaller exhibits within the context of these expositions brought together the latest decorative arts, painting and sculpture, much of which also bore close affinities to art deco. The expositions also distributed posters, written and pictorial materials, and other souvenirs that required the services of graphic designers and others to create appropriate designs. These expositions not only summed up contemporary artistic trends but, in a broader sense, expressed both implicitly and overtly the political and social concerns and aspirations of the times.

The 1925 Paris Exposition introduced art deco to the world. The French designers – who had adapted the German modernist ideas of the Munich *Werkbund*, combined them with motifs from cubism and the Russian ballet, and added abstract

Right: Berenice Abbott's *Manhattan Bridge, Looking Up,* ca. 1936-40.

Above: A poster for the 1933 World's Fair. The artist was Weimer Pursell.

Above right: A 1939 poster for the New York World's Fair of 1939-41, featuring the emblematic Trylon and Perisphere.

floral motifs derived from art nouveau – were the stars of the show with their virtuosity in furniture design, laquerwork, ceramics, glass, textiles, and metalwork. Especially outstanding was the furniture of Emile-Jacques Ruhlmann, the glass of René Lalique, and the metalwork of Edgar Brandt.

In its own expositions of the 1930s, the United States sought to equal and even surpass the Parisian venture. At the 1933 Chicago Century of Progress Exposition, architect Raymond Hood led the planning board, ably assisted by other art deco designers such as Harvey Wiley Corbett, Paul Philippe Cret, John Wellborn Root, Hubert Burnham, Lee Lawrie, Ralph T. Walker, Norman Bel Geddes, and Joseph Urban as the director of color. Regardless of the differing views on the fair's art deco architecture, the Chicago exposition offered a valuable opportunity to test new engineering techniques, construction materials, and building methods. At the time, the buildings were hailed as the ultimate in modernism, but only in retrospect did it become apparent that the architecture was fundamentally backward looking. It was closely tied to the polychromatic Parisian deco style of the 1920s, at a time when the streamline

style had become the trend of the future. Indeed, the streamline phase of art deco was introduced to the public at the Chicago fair in the form of an aerodynamic transport vehicle. The experimental version of the Burlington Zephyr, a high-speed train designed to travel at speeds of up to 100 miles per hour, made its debut in the fair's second season.

The two American expositions that occurred at the end of the decade in San Francisco and New York were quite different in intent and appearance. The 1939 Golden Gate International Exposition's exotic fantasy architecture evoked some vanished pre-Columbian paradise of Oceanic Shangri-la, an effect achieved through the display of stylized, primitive sculptures and Aztec style architecture.

The intent of the 1939 New York World of Tomorrow Fair was to investigate the idea of a totally planned environment that would be facilitated by technology, and symbolically realized through the use of streamlined style architecture and design. The roster of art deco participants was a most impressive one – Norman Bel Geddes, Henry Dreyfuss, Raymond Loewy, Walter Dorwin Teague, Egmont Arens, George Sakier, Gilbert Rohde, Donald Deskey, Russel Wright, Hugh Ferriss, Albert Kahn, Harvey Wiley Corbett, and Ely Jacques Kahn. Joseph Binder was commissioned to create the now classic art deco design that became one of the most widely distributed posters of modern times. The poster featured the symbol of the fair, a colossal cubist grouping of Trylon (triangular pylon) and Perisphere (a globe entered by the Helicline, a spiral ramp). Inside was Democracity, an enormous futuristic multimedia diorama. At the time, cultural commentator Lewis Mumford quipped that the Perisphere was a "great egg, out of which civilization is to be born."

Much thought by industrial designers had gone into planning the sequence of the buildings, effective pedestrian patterns, and psychologically compelling display techniques to promote the utopian ideas, technological advances, and new consumer products that were the fair's raison d'être. Such marvels as television, robots, a speech synthesizer, labor-saving household appliances, and superhighways persuaded many visitors that the World of Tomorrow was more than just an enticing vision and that the dreary depression years could not last forever. The New York World's Fair was, in effect, the grand finale of the art deco style. The exposition was the result of architects, designers, and artists working in collaboration as they had done on so many previous art deco projects. For one last time they represented in characteristic art deco symbolism America's love affair with the technology of the modern age, in the stylized transportation vehicles, bridges, radios, electric power networks and factories that decorated the wall surfaces. Mythic images of humans as supermen in the cosmos and as heroic laborers in the workplace were also present.

While the expositions proposed theoretical antidotes to the economic depression, far more practical and drastic measures were necessary to ward off total catastrophe. The 1929 stock market crash and the lean years that followed, in the United States and abroad, had effectively brought to an end the optimistic and extravagant phase of zigzag art deco. The skyscrapers still under construction were completed, but few major building projects would be forthcoming from the private sector for some time. To create jobs for the growing army of the unemployed, the federal government intervened. The result was a vast and unprecedented experiment in governmental patronage of the arts, as President Franklin Delano Roosevelt's New

Deal administration established a series of agencies to keep thousands of artists, designers, and architects gainfully employed. An implicit goal of these New Deal programs was to maintain political stability by engaging potential revolutionaries in a nationwide effort to forge a better society. This could be achieved only by making jobs widely available.

The most ambitious of the New Deal programs were the building projects. By the end of the 1930s, the nation had augmented its public building inventory by hundreds of new post offices, city halls, libraries, schools, court houses, and other civic structures. Although official policy did not dictate as to the architectural style of these Public Works Administration (PWA) buildings, they did possess, in retrospect – and with allowance for various colonial revival style exceptions – a remarkably uniform aspect. What emerged as the most popular style was classical moderne, the conservative variant of art deco. As a stylized adaptation of the architecture of ancient Greece and Rome and a direct descendant of eighteenth- and nineteenth-century neoclassicism, the style had been long considered suitable for civic buildings. Most of the major buildings projects, such as the new Oregon State Capitol, included a didactic program of appropriate artwork, incorporating such art deco motifs as skyscrapers, lightning bolts, and transportation themes, as seen in Waylande Gregory's sculpture, *Light Dispelling the Darkness*. The murals, following the lead of Diego Rivera and other members of the Mexican muralist movement, usually were historically relevant and socially charged.

The propagandist quality of New Deal art and architecture had much in common with that of totalitarian Europe, with such parallels as the symbolic use of monumental classical moderne architecture, the massive government building programs, the portrayal of heroic superman-like figures in painting and sculpture, and the romanticizing of labor. Links also existed between such specific symbols as the eagle of the Nazis and of the New Deal; and the lightning used by the Nazis to represent their storm troopers, and by the United States as an emblem of dynamic energy. The preoccupation of the totalitarians with psychological conditioning and behavioral control

Right: The Cord 810 Phaeton, 1936, built by Auburn Automobile Company. Gordon M. Buehrig was the designer.

reflected the interests of American industrial designers. Similarly, the totalitarian predilection for mass athletic displays of calisthenics carried on in mechanical unison had an American counterpart in the synchronized dance choreography of Busby Berkeley's musical films of the era.

The 1930s were a chaotic and unpredictable decade. The response of both the democracies and the fascist states was to use classical moderne architecture to project an image of power and stability, and to employ surprisingly similar imagery to promote solutions to the era's problems. The result, in design terms, was the end of art deco. By now the grim connotation of authoritarian regimentation had subsumed the joyous optimism of the roaring 1920s. The devaluation of the symbolism of art deco was complete.

By the end of the 1930s, the design and manufacture of art deco artifacts and buildings had come to a virtual standstill. The onset of World War II demanded that industry shift its full capacity to the production of military material and armaments. In the postwar decades, the stripped purity of the international style came to rule the urban skyline and to dominate as the fashionable ideal of American design. The economy of erecting multitudes of almost identical boxes of glass, steel, and concrete was undeniable. And further, the international style's ideological underpinning – a utopian socialism – were appropriate as well to the tide of progress that swept away the shabby and old-fashioned vestiges of earlier times in the name of urban renewal. All too often, unfortunately, the buildings leveled by the wrecker's ball included quirky, extravagant, and by now outmoded examples of the art deco style.

Eventually the wheel of fashion turned, forestalling the extinction of the art deco style. The 1960s, a decade of social and political upheaval, saw an artistic revolution as well. The pop art movement forcefully challenged abstraction as the sanctioned mode of visual expression and returned representative

imagery to the forefront of the avant-garde. A landmark event was the 1966 Paris exhibition, *Les Années 25, Art Deco/Bauhaus/Stijl/Esprit Nouveau*, which dared the previously unimaginable. Art deco, long scorned for its fussy ornamentalism and crass commercialism by academics and by functionalist architects and designers, now was treated as a twentieth-century design movement of respectable stature.

The revival of art deco that followed spread quickly and widely, carried as it was on a wave of popular nostalgia for more glamorous times. Numerous exhibitions subsequently focused on the style as a whole, its various phases and aspects, and on the work of individual designers. The result was a plethora of exhibit catalogs, newspaper, magazine and journal articles, and books. What began as a popular revival led by collectors and graphic designers inevitably attracted intellectual scrutiny and analysis.

Robert Venturi's influential 1966 book, *Complexity and Contradiction in Architecture*, constructed a theoretical framework for the adaptation and inclusion of varied historical and vernacular styles in a contemporary context. With his witty transmutation of the functionalist motto of "less is more" into "less is a bore," Venturi led the way to postmodernism, the predominant architectural and design movement of the 1980s. Central to Venturi's ideas and to postmodernism was a renewed attention to the symbolic meanings and cultural context of architecture. Like art deco, postmodernism characteristically incorporated color, ornament, and historical motifs from varied sources in symbolic ways or ironic combinations. For a number of commissions, postmodernism architects turned to art deco as a model, using such elements as its abstracted monumentality, bright colors, horizontal banding, unusual materials, decorative glass and lighting fixtures, skyscraper style setbacks, cubistic columns, geometric ornament, and stylized sculpture. In its sophisticated combination of stylistic allu-

Left: Ruby Keeler and a "dancing" art deco skyline in *Forty-second Street*, 1933.

Right: The Coulters Building, ca. 1939, a fine art deco structure that has since been demolished.

Below right: This dining room in a private residence on Grosse Isle, MI, is a fine example of art deco revival.

sions, postmodernism shared not only the forms of art deco but also something of its spirit.

A leading force in the appropriation of art deco in post-modernism was architect Michael Graves, not only with such buildings as the Plocek house and the city office building of Portland, Oregon, but also in his furniture designs, as well as in his "Big Dipper" coffee set and his idiosyncratic and architectonic silver tea and coffee set for Alessi. Other architects open to the allure of art deco included Richard Meier with his streamline style High Museum of Art in Atlanta, and Kohn Pedersen Fox Associates with their design for the world headquarters of Proctor & Gamble with its zigzag style setbacks.

Nor was the art deco revival limited to postmodern adaptations. It also was an essential factor in the historic preservation and restoration of such monuments of art deco architecture as Radio City Music Hall, the Oakland Paramount Theater, and Cincinnati's Union Terminal. Unfortunately, other such art deco gems as Joseph Urban's Ziegfeld Theater and the Atlantic Richfield Oil Company Building in Los Angeles had been razed in the meantime. A key victory by preservationists was the 1979 official designation of one square mile of old Miami Beach, comprising some 400 primarily tropical deco structures, as a historic district by the National Registry of Historic Places. The preservation movement also led in the attempt to document by means of photographs, pamphlets, articles, catalogs and books specific art deco buildings. As a result there are now surveys of the art deco architecture of Manhattan, the Bronx, Washington, Baltimore, Seattle, Los Angeles, Tulsa, Pittsburgh, Miami Beach, Vermont, and the Southwest; as well as studies of such major buildings as the Oakland Paramount, the Louisiana State Capitol, and the crown jewel of American art deco, Rockefeller Center. Facilitating the efforts of the preservationists were the recently established art deco societies, many of which circulated newsletters and hosted walking tours and symposia.

On the leading edge of the art deco revival in the visual arts were the graphic designers, although craftspeople and industrial designers were not far behind. The lively glamor of art deco motifs appealed to such prominent designers as Milton Glaser, Seymour Chwast, and Norman Green who adapted art deco's vividly colored geometric patterns for posters, book jackets, record album covers, and advertisements. As the revival stretched into the 1980s, graphic designers came to use such specific art deco imagery as Cassandre-like looming ocean liners, dramatically silhouetted skyscraper skylines, DC-8 propeller planes, streamlined locomotives, palm trees, flamingos, and sleekly stylized human and animal figures. The revival provided a rich new source of ideas for designers too young to remember the art deco decades but who nevertheless were charmed by its nostalgic imagery.

In the area of furniture and interior design, the revival encouraged manufacturers during the 1980s to reissue various classics of art deco furniture. Among these pieces were a number of chairs and tables by Eliel Saarinen, as well as the work of such Europeans as Josef Hoffmann, René Herbst, Robert Mallet-Stevens, and Elaine Gray. Beginning in the late 1970s such fine furniture artisans as Judy Kensley McKie and Wendell

Castle produced one-of-a-kind pieces that bore close affinities to the art deco style. Postmodern pieces in the art deco mode for manufacture were designed by Venturi, Graves, and Chwast. As in the art deco decades, multitalented architects – including Venturi, Graves, Meier, Laurinda Spear, Stanley Tigerman, and Robert Stern – were encouraged to create designs for china, silverware, and household accessories. At the same time, Noritake resumed production of Frank Lloyd Wright's china for the Tokyo Imperial Hotel, and the recently reprieved Radio City Music Hall became the source of twenty textile designs adapted from its original archives. Steuben Glass continued to produce its 1930s art deco designs by Sidney Waugh and others.

For interior designers in search of sophisticated glamor, the art deco style provided a rich lode. Striking effects were achieved by using authentic historical architectural elements such as sculpture, doors, etched glass, stained glass windows, and even entire rooms that had been rescued from demolished

Below: Atlanta's High Museum of Art, 1985, by Richard Meier.

Right: The Rainbow Room in New York City after it was reworked in the 1980s.

buildings. Unexpected but effective uses of art deco artifacts have included the installation of an art deco Loew's theater marquee over a bar, and the display of two stone eagles from New York's late Airlines Terminal Building as the guardians at the entrance of a Virginia corporate headquarters.

A major project of art deco revival interior design was the 1988 renovation of Rockfeller Center's fabled Rainbow Room restaurant. Hugh Hardy sympathetically updated the club with such new elements as cabinetry designed in homage to Donald Deskey. This ambitious collaborative effort resulted in a theatrical interplay of light, glass, and mirror in a sumptuous setting of terrazzo, cast glass, and mahogany. The dominating icon was a Norman Bel Geddes aerodynamic model of a streamlined ocean liner mounted over the south bar.

Perhaps it is ironic that the art deco style in revival form appealed so strongly to the creative and commercial vanguard of the 1980s. The more opulent projects, such as the Rainbow Room, had a money-is-no-object aura about them that was all too reminiscent of the 1920s. The 1920s and the 1980s had much in common after all. These decades shared a boundless optimism, an acceptance of hedonism as a guiding principle of life, the free expression of materialistic excess, and the glorification of expansive wealth. Surely no style was more appropriate to such times than art deco.

William Van Alen
Chrysler Building, 1930
New York, NY
Photo: Rainbow/Larry Brownstein

ARCHITECTURE

A virtual flowering of art deco architecture occurred in the United States. America led the way in the large number of buildings erected, in the sheer exuberance of their ornament in the number of architects working successfully in this style, and in the range of regional and stylistic variants explored. While the major modernist innovations leading to art deco took place in Glasgow, Helsinki, and Vienna, in America, shortly after 1900, Frank Lloyd Wright's proto-art deco Larkin Company Building and Unity Temple were completed. Deeply interested in symbolic architecture, integrated ornament, and total design of interiors, Wright went on to work in the Aztec style, using geometrically patterned textile block in such California masterpieces as the Barnsdall, Millard, Storer, Freeman, and Ennis houses. In the 1930s, he completed the Johnson Wax complex, now widely acknowledged as a high point of the streamline style.

Characteristic of the roaring twenties, the flamboyant jazzy version of art deco known as the skyscraper or zigzag style was relatively short-lived, lasting from 1925 to 1931. The actual form the skyscraper took was determined by a 1916 New York City zoning ordinance that mandated building setbacks, leading to a stepped-back contour. The other decisive factor was Eliel Saarinen's second place entry in the 1922 Chicago Tribune Tower competition, liberating the skyscraper from strict reliance on historical styles and pointing the way toward a modernistic abstraction. The result was buildings embellished with picturesque ornament in a rich variety of materials. The opulent entrances, lobbies, elevators, and even mailboxes were all part of the total coordinated design, often realized through the collaboration of designers, artists, and craftspeople.

In 1923 construction began on New York's first zigzag building, Ralph Walker's Barclay-Vesey (or New York Telephone) Building. One of the most talented and productive of Manhattan's art deco architects was Ely Jacques Kahn, who designed over thirty such structures. The first actual skyscraper in the zigzag style was Sloan & Robertson's luxurious Chanin Building. The archetypal art deco skyscraper was William Van Alen's dramatic Chrysler Building with its fantastic soaring spire; and the Empire State Building, topped with a machine age mooring mast for dirigibles, provided a fitting end to the heroic era of the art deco skyscraper. Zigzag deco spread nationwide, with important buildings rising in Pittsburgh, Kansas City, Tulsa, and elsewhere. Southern California, which underwent a period of remarkable prosperity and growth in the 1920s, was the site of a number of exotic variations on zigzag deco and related stlyes. Throughout the art deco era, the stylized, dignified neoclassicism of classical moderne remained a conservative option, though often with surprisingly flamboyant interiors for banks and other public buildings. Paul Philippe Cret was a leading architect of this style.

The 1929 stock market crash abruptly ended the optimistic era of the ostentatious zigzag style architecture. From now on the key was to be austerity, and the result was the third distinctive manifestation of art deco known as the streamline style, which featured aerodynamic curves, flat roofs, glass brick, banded windows, tubular steel railings, and horizontal speed stripes. The style first appeared in Raymond Hood's McGraw-Hill Building with its streamlined base and lobby. Raymond Hood also collaborated with a large group of architects on the design of Rockefeller Center, now considered one of the greatest achievements of American art deco.

Although never widely favored for domestic housing, in its more picturesque form the streamline style became a popular choice for commercial clients such as Coca Cola, which commissioned Robert Derrah to transform its Los Angeles bottling plant with portholes and a ship's bridge and other nautical details of the "steamship style." In Florida the streamline style combined with zigzag motifs and regional imagery to produce the tropical deco of Miami Beach. The futuristic streamline style climaxed at the 1939 New York World's Fair.

The widest application of the streamline style was seen in smaller commercial buildings. Not only was it used for modest sometimes prefabricated roadside structures such as gas stations, diners, bus terminals and stores, but from 1936 on, it was often utilized in the context of the "modernize Main Street" movement. This led to the renovation of countless traditionally styled commercial structures, which were covered over with modernistic facades using such machine age materials as vitrolite, black glass, colored enameled panels, aluminum, and plastic, along with neon tube lighting. Not only the streamline style, but also the zigzag style were used in these image transformations in an attempt to attract more business. Eventually the streamline style became a well-established commercial style of the 1940s and 1950s.

RIGHT:
Martin Theater, Panama City, FL
Photo: © John Margolies/Esto. All rights reserved.

West Theater, Cedartown, GA
Photo: © John Margolies/Esto. All rights reserved.

Hood & Fouilhoux and Reinhard & Hofmester and
Corbett, Harrison & MacMurray
Rockefeller Center, 1932-40
New York, NY
Photo: © Ezra Stoller/Esto. All rights reserved.

LEFT:
Smith, Hinchman and Grylls
Guardian Building, 1929, Detroit, MI
Photo: © Balthazar Korab Ltd.

Guardian Building (detail), 1929, Detroit, MI
Photo: © Balthazar Korab Ltd.

Tropical deco architecture, Miami Beach, FL
Photo: Steven Brooke

LEFT:
Tropical deco building, Miami, FL
Photo: © Tim Street-Porter/Esto. All rights reserved.

Berkeley Shore Building, Miami, FL
Photo: © Tim Street-Porter/Esto. All rights reserved.

Streamline-style Diner
Photo: © John Margolies/Esto. All rights reserved.

Streamline-style Diner, St. Paul, MN
Photo: © John Margolies/Esto. All rights reserved.

Entrance, Rockefeller Center, New York, NY
Photo: © Ezra Stoller/Esto. All rights reserved.

34

Frank Lloyd Wright
S.C. Johnson and Son Administration Building, 1936,
and Research Tower, 1944
Racine, WI
Photo courtesy of Johnson Wax

RIGHT
Frank Lloyd Wright
Charles Ennis Residence, 1923
Los Angeles, CA
Photo: © Balthazar Korab Ltd.

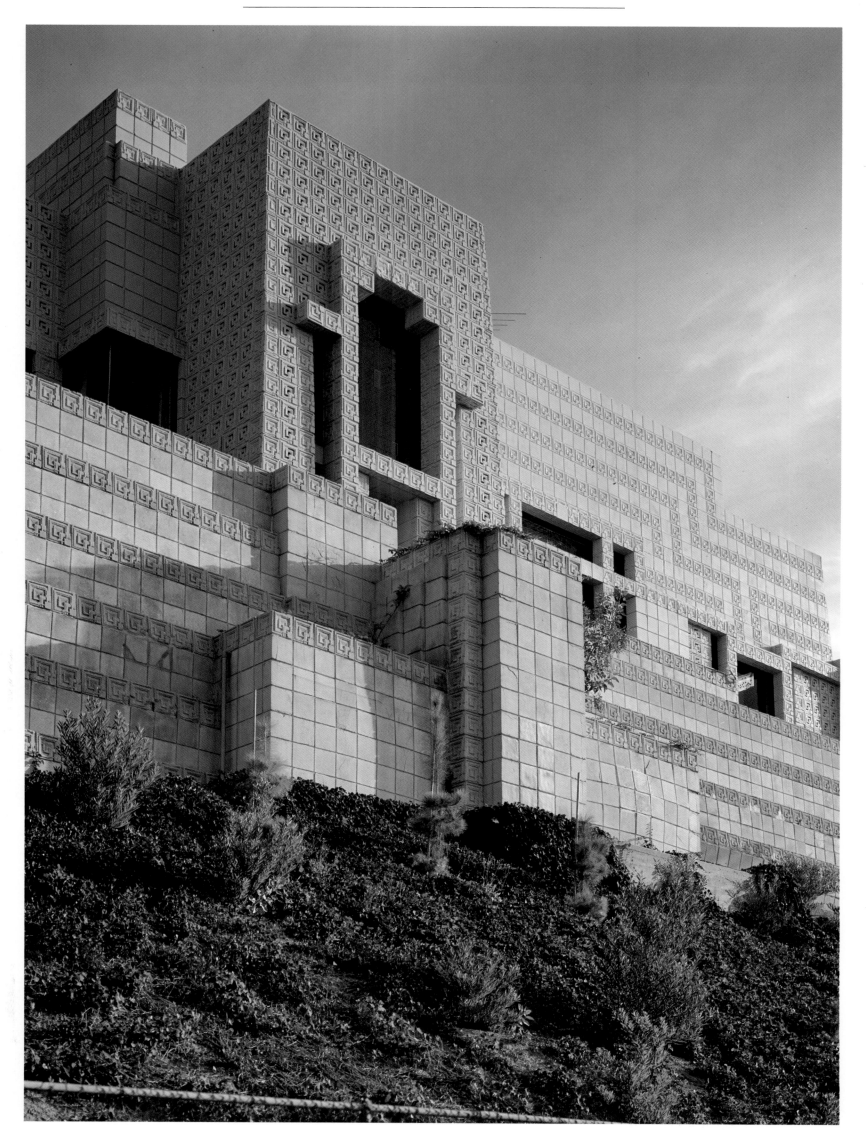

Eliel Saarinen
Exterior, Cranbrook Academy of Art, 1925
Bloomfield Hills, MI
Photo: © Balthazar Korab Ltd.

OVERLEAF:
Exterior details, Chanin Building in foreground,
Chrysler Building in background.
New York, NY
Photo: Susan Bernstein

Bley & Lyman, consultants to King & King
Niagara Hudson (now Niagara Mohawk) Building, 1932
Syracuse, NY
Photo: © *Stuart Lisson*

RIGHT:
Shreve, Lamb & Harmon
Empire State Building, 1931
New York, NY
Photo: © *Peter Mauss/Esto. All rights reserved.*

Donald Deskey (supervisor)
Interior, Radio City Music Hall
New York, NY
Photo: © Ezra Stoller/Esto. All rights reserved.

Furniture and Design

Although French skill in art deco furniture and interior design is widely acknowledged, historically German and Austrian modernism reached the United States decades earlier. The Munich style was seen in Bruno Paul's furniture at the 1904 St. Louis Fair, and immigrant designers helped to disseminate the style here. From the Vienna Werkstätte came Joseph Urban in 1911 and Paul Frankl in 1914, while the newest German ideas arrived with Winold Reiss in 1913 and in 1914 with Kem Weber.

Some of the first truly modern pieces of furniture, certainly akin to art deco, were dreamed up by Frank Lloyd Wright. Wright was as much a virtuoso in interior and furniture design as he was in architecture, being as he was a pioneering advocate of the interior unified by design – a concept central to art deco. Thus he designed coordinating furniture, light fixtures, textiles, wall treatments, and geometrically stylized leaded glass windows suited to a specific structure. Some of Wright's inventive designs important to art deco include the zigzag style chairs for the Tokyo Imperial Hotel, and the streamlined desk and chairs for the Johnson Wax Building.

Apart from Wright's activity, a major impetus for art deco furniture design came from Europe. An influx of immigrant designers, which included Eliel Saarinen, William Lescaze, Ilonka Karasz, and Walter von Nessen, provided the leaders of a movement that sought to transform the fashionable public and domestic environment. Concurrently, many leading American-born designers – among them, Donald Deskey, Gilbert Rohde, Eugene Schoen, Ruth Reeves, Raymond Hood, and Ely Jacques Kahn – either traveled or studied in Europe, becoming familiar there with the latest design ideas.

A selection of works from the 1925 Paris Exposition later traveled to New York's Metropolitan Museum of Art and to eight other museums. Although specialty shops and galleries already had made the French and Austrian high styles available in the United States, now department stores began to exhibit, commission, and promote modernist design. The first major, uniquely American exhibit was that hosted by the Metropolitan Museum of Art in an attempt to foster collaboration between designers and industry. The 1929 *Architect and the Industrial Arts* featured thirteen-room ensembles created by leading architects, among them Ely Jacques Kahn, Ralph Walker, Joseph Urban, Eugene Schoen, John Wellborn Root,

Eliel Saarinen, and Raymond Hood. These versatile architects designed not only the integrated modernist furniture and accessories, but also the textiles and geometric wall treatments.

The stylistic sources of American art deco furniture in the 1920s were diverse. From the neoclassical and empire styles came the refined use of contrasting veneers, fluting, octagonal and oval forms, sunburst and fan-shaped motifs, and pedestal bases. From Chinese furniture came the low center of gravity and the use of black and lacquered finishes. From the machine aesthetic came the use of industrial materials such as chromium, aluminum, and bakelite. From cubism came the angular, sculptural shapes and the use of vibrant colors and geometric ornament. From primitivism came the use of exotic woods and other unusual natural materials.

The most distinctive motif of the era was the stepped skyscraper style enthusiastically promoted and produced by Paul Frankl in the form of desks, bookcases, and dressing tables. Even more dramatically zigzag was a furniture suite created by Abel Faidy. Some of the most elegant pieces were those designed by Saarinen. Shortly after his arrival from Finland, Saarinen became involved with the establishment, design, and directorship of the Cranbrook Academy of Art outside Detroit. Cranbrook's resident artists were to become a source of sophisticated modernist design in all media.

With the Wall Street crash came a repudiation of the luxurious 1920s style, and a turn toward a more functionalist aesthetic, which continued the use of machine age materials such as plastic, glass, and industrial metals, but in a more purely structural way rather than ornamentally. The streamline phase of art deco, promoted by the rising generation of industrial designers, came to dominate 1930s design with its rounded contours and horizontal speed stripes. It was also a style more suited to mass production and hence to the limited economic expectations of these years.

The seductive quality of the art deco environment was recognized quickly by commercial patrons of the style. Many restaurants, nightclubs, shops, hotels, and ocean liners were infused with art deco. The best-known art deco environment, of course, was that created for Rockefeller Center, its highlight being the coordinated interior design of Radio City Music Hall, supervised by Donald Deskey. Radio City, the last of the palatial movie theaters, provided a fitting end to the era.

Donald Deskey (supervisor)
Powder Room, Radio City Music Hall
New York, NY
Photo: © Peter Aaron/Esto. All rights reserved.

Eliel Saarinen
Armchairs and Table for Saarinen House, 1929-31
Collection of Cranbrook Academy of Art Museum
Photo courtesy of The Detroit Institute of Arts

Eliel Saarinen
Dining Room, Saarinen House, 1928-30
Bloomfield Hills, MI
Photo: © Balthazar Korab Ltd.

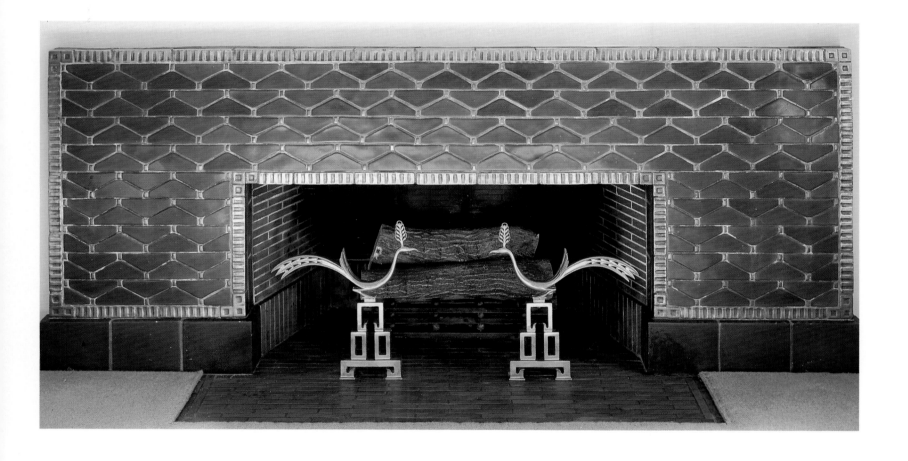

Eliel Saarinen
Peacock and andirons for Saarinen House
Photo: Dirk Bakker/Cranbrook Academy of Art Museum

Eliel Saarinen
Interior, Living Room, Saarinen House, 1928-30
Photo: © Balthazar Korab Ltd.

Frank Lloyd Wright
Johnson Wax Administration Building, 1936
Great Workroom in 1939
Racine, WI
Photo courtesy of Johnson Wax

RIGHT:
Abel Faidy
Skyscraper-style Armchair, 1927
Photo: Chicago Historical Society

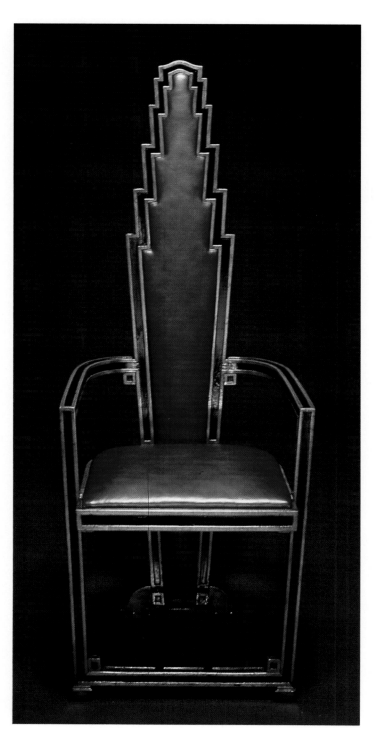

ABOVE:
Frank Lloyd Wright
Desk and Chair for Johnson Wax Administration Building
Photo courtesy of Steelcase, Inc.

LEFT:
Donald Deskey
Three Leaf Screen, ca. 1929
oil paint and metal leaf on canvas, wood
Gift of Sidney and Francis Lewis
Virginia Museum of Fine Arts
Richmond, VA

Charles Baskerville
Rocky Mountain Goats Screen, 1936
Lacquer on masonite
Gift of Charles Payson
Courtesy Cooper-Hewitt National Museum of Design
Smithsonian Institution/Art Resources, New York, NY

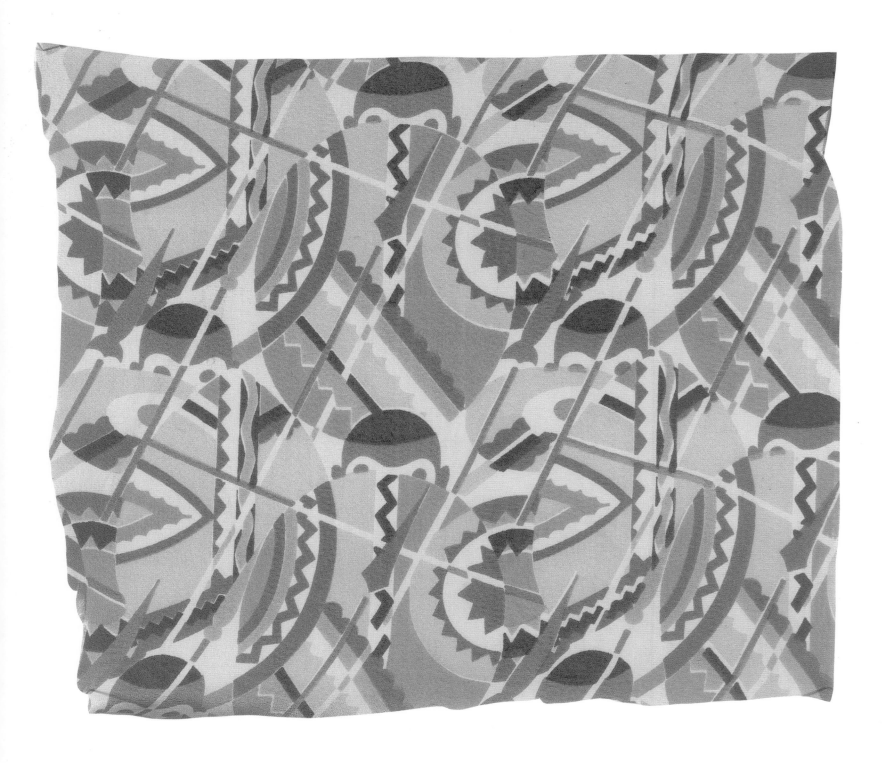

LEFT:
Lillian Holm
First Sight of New York, wall hanging
Gift of the artist in memory of Ralph T. Sayles
Flint Institute of Arts, Flint, MI

Frederick Suhr for Belding Heminway
Safari Series, 1929, textile
Printed on crepe-de-chine
Purchase 1930, Collection of The Newark Museum,
Newark, NJ

Rene Clark for Stehli Silks
Stadium, 1927 (detail), textile
printed crepe-de-chine silk
*Purchase 1927, Collection of The Newark Museum,
Newark, NJ*

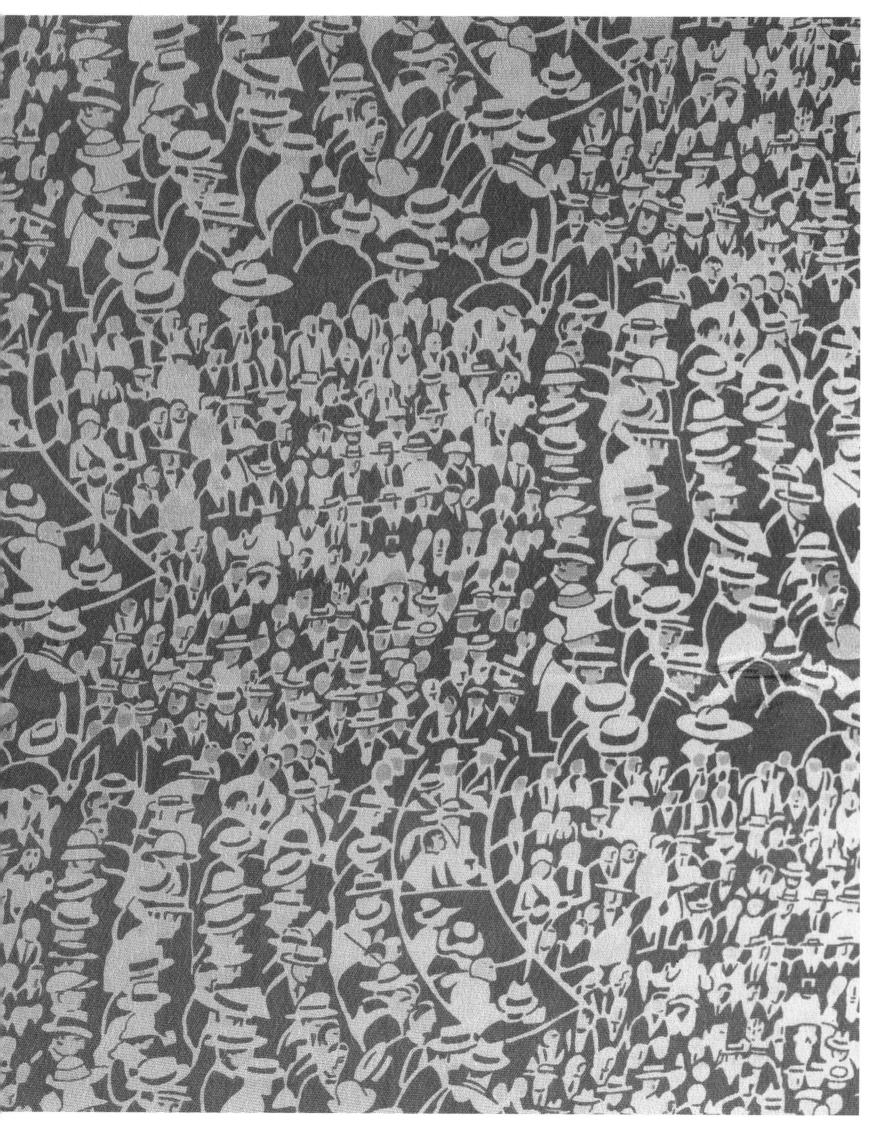

LEFT:
Frank Lloyd Wright
Tree of Life, window
Martin House, 1904
Art Institute of Chicago

Smith, Hinchman and Grylls
Interior, Guardian Building, 1929, Detroit, MI
Photo: © Balthazar Korab Ltd.

ABOVE RIGHT:
Frank Lloyd Wright
Glass mural, Grand Lobby, Arizona Biltmore
Phoenix, AZ
Photo: © Balthazar Korab Ltd.

BELOW RIGHT:
Frank Lloyd Wright
Facade detail, Arizona Biltmore
Phoenix, AZ
Photo: © Balthazar Korab Ltd.

John Held Jr. for Stehli Silks
Rhapsody, detail, 1929, textile
printed on crepe-de-chine
*Purchase 1928, Collection of The Newark Museum,
Newark, NJ*

Interior detail, Chanin Building, 1926-29
New York, NY
Photo: Susan Bernstein

RIGHT:
Jacques Delamarre
Executive bathroom, Chanin Building, 1929
New York, NY
Photo: Angelo Hornak

Chicago World's Fair 1933 Poster
Chicago Historical Society

THE VISUAL ARTS

The totally designed art deco environment required appropriate decoration in the form of sculpture and painting. The deco variant of these arts was distinct from the works of avant-garde artists not only in that it was a more conservative adaptation of modernist trends, but also in that it was an art primarily intended to embellish architectural surfaces and settings. Thus art deco sculpture includes the reliefs adorning building interiors and exteriors, and freestanding statues, as well as the sculpture produced for monuments, memorials, fountains, gardens, and parks. Similarly, art deco painting primarily refers to murals, panels, and screens, and may also include works preferred or commissioned by interior decorators.

Frank Lloyd Wright led in the American use of geometrically stylized sculpture, sometimes after his own design. To this end, he worked closely with sculptors Richard Bock and Alfonso Iannelli. Some of the era's leading sculptors were able to balance avant-garde experiment with public commissions in the art deco style. John Storrs produced cubist figural studies and abstract "skyscraper" sculpture, as well as such public monuments as the streamlined colossus Ceres, the "ultimate art deco goddess." Equally versatile was Isamu Noguchi, who came from study with Gutzon Borglum of Mount Rushmore fame, to sculpt a gleaming machinelike portrait head of Buckminster Fuller and a ten-ton stainless steel relief of heroic newspaper workers for the Associated Press Building.

The "dean" of American architectural sculptors was Lee Lawrie, who worked on Goodhue's Nebraska State Capitol, Chicago's "Fountain of Time" and Rockefeller Center's Atlas. Rockefeller Center was an important patron of such sculptors as Paul Manship, an accomplished maker of elegant reinterpretations from classical mythology. The era's building boom kept busy an army of art deco sculptors, including Sidney Waugh, Carl Paul Jennewein, Edmond Amateis, Leo Friedlander, René Paul Chambellan, Lorado Taft, John Gregory, and Edgar Miller. For the interior, smaller tabletop sculptures included Amazon women, flappers, dancers and acrobats, as well as such animals as greyhounds and gazelles. The more talented makers of such works included Alexander Archipenko, Elie Nadelman, Gaston Lachaise, Boris Lovet-Lorski, W. H. Diederich, Robert Laurent, and William Zorach.

In painting, a conservative approach to avant-garde ideas also marked the work of leading American painters. Max Weber's, Man Ray's, and H. Lyman Säyen's interpretation of cubism; Joseph Stella's version of futurism; and Louis Lozowick's constructivist creations all were markedly decorative, as were the paintings and murals of such regionalists as Grant Wood and Thomas Hart Benton, and of their more urban cousins, the precisionists – including the skyscraper, bridge, and factory portraits by Charles Sheeler, Elsie Driggs, and Georgia O'Keeffe.

Painted screens often accessorized art deco interiors. Among the more prolific in this area were Robert Winthrop Chanler, whose best work depicted stylized tropical scenes, and Charles Baskerville, who completed many screens and murals for private houses as well as for the ship SS America.

Theaters, nightclubs, hotels, and restaurants provided employment for decorative muralists, as did Rockefeller Center and the expositions. Leaders in the field included Hildreth Meire, Winold Reiss, Witold Gordon, Ezra Winter, Henry Billings, Boardman Johnson, Yasuo Kuniyoshi, Alfred Tulk, and Pierre Bourdelle. The 1930s brought a more serious tone to the murals. Inspired by Mexican muralist Diego Rivera, New Deal artists provided post offices, schools, hospitals, and other public buildings with some 4,000, often didactic and nationalistic, murals celebrating civic virtues and traditional values.

In the area of graphic art and illustration, the American contribution was bolstered by the fine work of visiting and immigrant European designers, such as Joseph Binder. The leading book illustrators, Rockwell Kent, John Vassos, and Lynd Ward, worked primarily in black and white. The film and theater posters of the era were fairly conservative in techniques, even when they used art deco imagery. American magazine illustrators such as John Held, Helen Dryden, Rita Senger, E. M. A. Steinmetz, Neysa McMein, Ilonka Karasz, George Wolf Plank, Gordon Conway, and Fish produced the most characteristic works of the 1920s style.

The finest body of 1930s graphic work was the output of the New Deal's WPA poster project, which issued some 35,000 designs for a wide range of government agencies to promote social causes, cultural events, tourism and, at the end of the decade and into the next, war propaganda. Of these posters, many of the more effective ones reflected the art deco style in both their technique and their subject matter, with such motifs as aerodynamic transport vehicles and heroic workers.

Heinz Warneke
Wild Boars, 1930
National Museum of American Art, Washington, D.C./
Art Resources, New York, NY

Carl Walters
Walrus, 1933, ceramic
National Museum of American Art, Washington, D.C./
Art Resources, New York, NY

High Voltage Railway Electrification, panel
1933, artist unknown
The Mitchell Wolfson, Jr. Collection, courtesy,
The Wolfsonian Foundation, Miami, FL

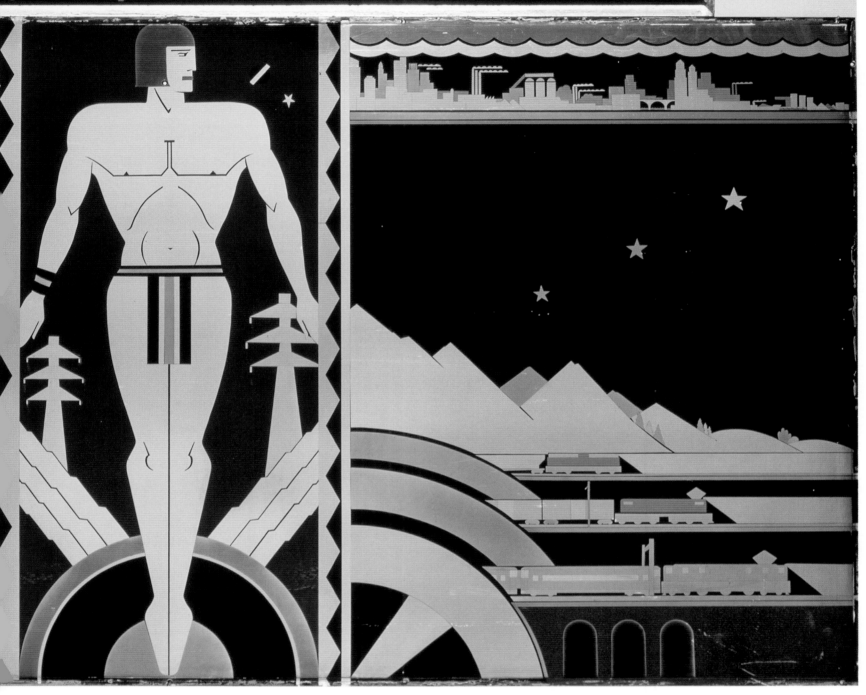

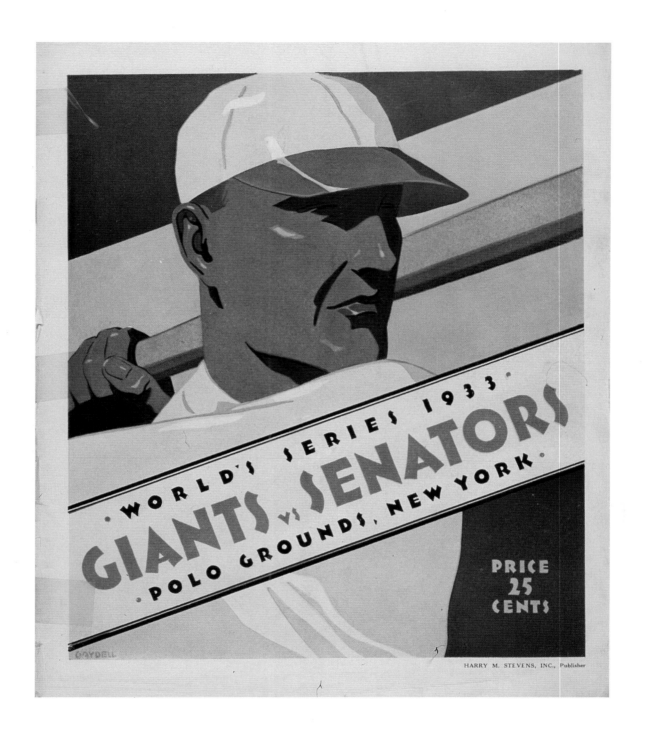

RIGHT:
Joseph Binder
Fortune: Vol XVI, No. 6, December 1937
The Mitchell Wolfson, Jr. Collection, courtesy
The Wolfsonian Foundation, Miami, FL

Program for the 1933 World Series
National Baseball Library, Cooperstown, NY

Paul Manship
Diana, 1925, bronze
Gift of Paul Manship
National Museum of American Art, Washington, D.C./
Art Resources, New York, NY

Paul Manship
Actaeon, 1925, bronze
Gift of Paul Manship
National Museum of American Art, Washington, D.C./
Art Resources, New York, NY

OVERLEAF:
Grant Wood
Overmantel Decoration
1930, oil on upsom board, 41×63¼in.
Gift of Isabel R. Stamats in memory of
Herbert S. Stamats, 1973
© *Cedar Rapids Museum of Art*

Peter Berent
6th Avenue El
ca. 1938, oil, masonite, 63×35¾in.
The Mitchell Wolfson, Jr. Collection, courtesy,
The Wolfsonian Foundation, Miami, FL

RIGHT:
Chicago "Boul Mich" by the Elevated Line
Photo: Chicago Historical Society

Grant Wood
Death on the Ridge Road
1935, oil on masonite panel, 32×39in.
Gift of Cole Porter
Williams College Museum of Art, Williamstown, MA

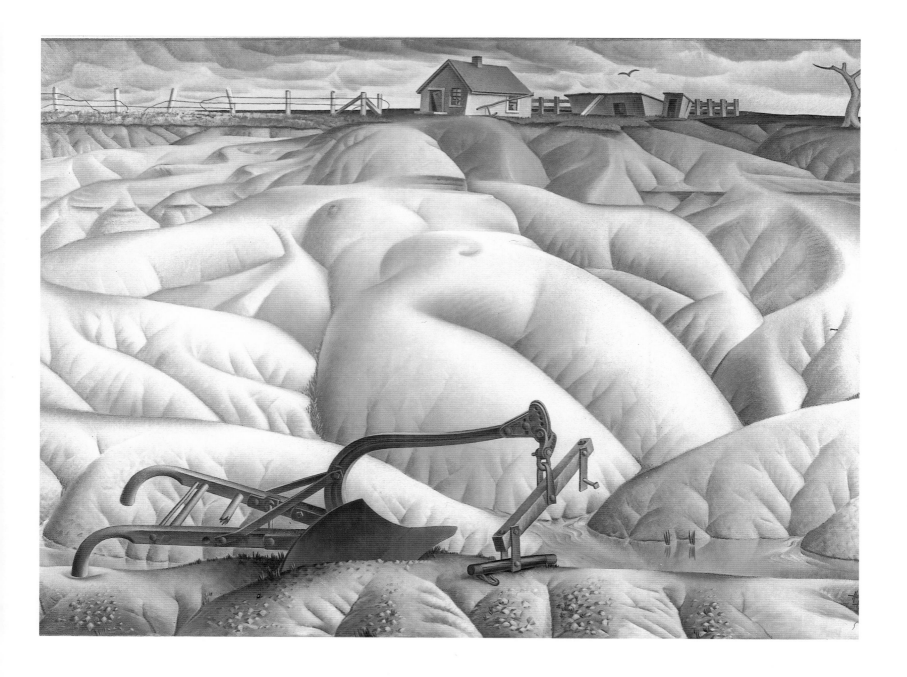

Alexandre Hogue
Erosion No. 2 – Mother Earth Laid Bare
1936, oil on canvas
The Philbrook Museum of Art, Tulsa, OK

81

82

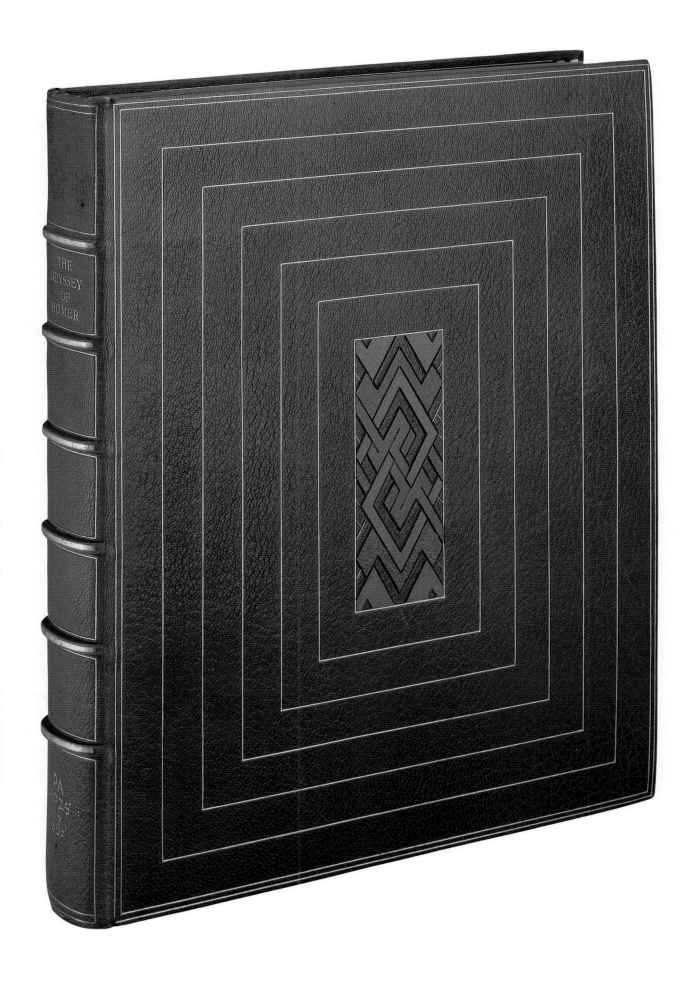

LEFT:
Jean Eschmann
Binding for the Odyssey of Homer
1931, tooled leather
Collection of The Cranbrook Academy of Art/Museum
Photograph courtesy of The Detroit Institute of Arts

Paul Fehér
Screen
1930, wrought iron with aluminum and brass plate applications
Designed for Rose Iron Works Inc., now
Rose Metal Industries, Cleveland, OH
Photo: © Randy Duster

Joseph Stella
The Voice of the City of New York Interpreted:
The Skyscrapers
1920-22, oil and tempera on canvas, 99¾×54in.
Purchase 1927, Felix Fuld Bequest Fund,
Collection of the Newark Museum, Newark, NJ

RIGHT:
Georgia O'Keeffe
New York, Night
1928-29, oil on canvas, 40⅛×19⅛in.
Thomas C. Woods Memorial Collection 1958
Sheldon Memorial Art Gallery
University of Nebraska, Lincoln, NB

Waylande de Santis Gregory
Europa and the Bull
1938, unglazed earthenware
Gift of the artist
Everson Museum of Art, Syracuse, NY
Photograph: © *1983 Bob Pike*

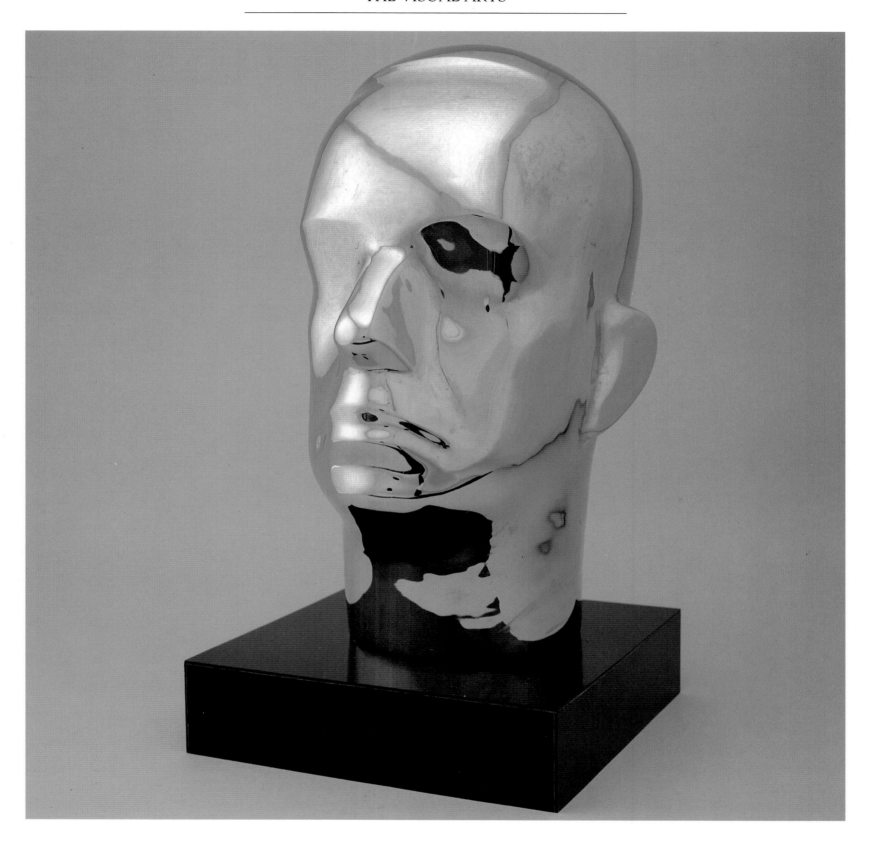

Isamu Noguchi
Portrait head of Buckminster Fuller
1929, chrome-plated bronze
University Museum, Southern Illinois University,
Carbondale, IL

Artist unknown
Poster for Federal Dance Theatre,
Library of Congress Federal Theatre Project Collection
at George Mason University Library, Fairfax, VA

RIGHT:
Artist unknown
Poster for Federal Dance Theatre,
Library of Congress Federal Theatre Project Collection
at George Mason University Library, Fairfax, VA

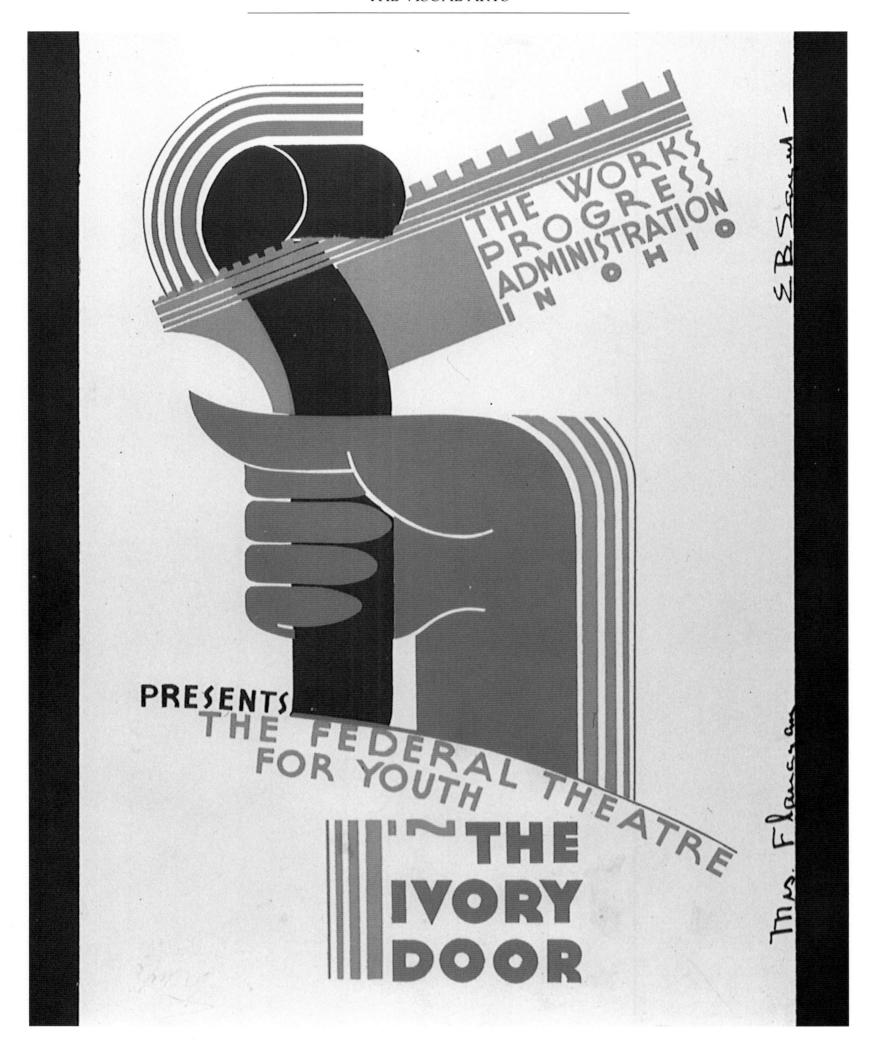

Sidney Waugh for Steuben Glass
Atlantica
1938-39, colorless glass
Gift of the Corning Glass Works
The Corning Museum of Glass, Corning, NY

90

THE USEFUL ARTS

The designs that traveled to the United States from the 1925 Paris Exposition found favor with the fashionable and wealthy, and soon American companies and immigrant designers stepped in to meet the demand by producing items for all pocketbooks.

This is certainly true of art deco glass, which reached the well-off in exquisite pieces by Frederick Carder of Steuben Glass. Quick to follow new trends, Carder turned from art nouveau to art deco with such Parisian motifs as crisply stylized foliage or leaping gazelles. Still later from Steuben came Sidney Waugh's mythological and astrological streamline style bowls. Catering to the other end of the economic spectrum were the producers of Depression glass. These dinnerware sets were sold at a very low cost, or even were given away by the piece at cinema "dish nights." Produced in a variety of color and patterns, the molded machine-made glass came in traditional styles, as well as in a limited number of art deco patterns. The most characteristic included the opaque Platonite Ovide; the zigzag style Pyramid, Sierra, Tea Room, and Ruba Rhombic; and the streamline style Ring, Circle, Manhattan, and Moderntone.

In the area of ceramics, a similar range of items reached the consumer. Attractive art deco designs came from such leading midwestern pottery works as Rookwood, Overbeck, Weller, Cowan, and Rosewood. In 1928, New York's Metropolitan Museum of Art introduced sophisticated figural works from the Vienna Werkstätte, leading many Americans to study there. The most famous of these, Viktor Schreckengost, later produced a notable series of punch bowls representing New Year's Eve in New York City. Other important ceramists of the era included Austrian emigré Vally Wieselthier, Cowan Pottery's Waylande Gregory, and Cranbrook Academy's Maija Grotell. Native American potters of the Southwest – foremost among them were Maria Martinez, Tonita and Juan Roybal, Nampayo and Lucy Lewis – made wares whose geometric Hopi, Pueblo, and Zuni designs of stylized bird, deer, flower, cloud, and lightning motifs fit in the art deco canon. The relatively inexpensive Noritake art deco porcelains – designed in New York and mass produced in Japan – employed probably the greatest range of art deco imagery, from conventionalized flowers and animals, geometric designs, stylized flappers, and exotic vistas, to vignettes of party life. But the most widely available art deco wares were the vividly colored, geometrically contoured, streamline striped dinner sets known as Fiesta and Harlequin. Bright colors and dramatic silhouettes also were a feature of bakelite items, which were made of the first completely synthetic plastic. Bakelite was used for radio cabinets, powder compacts, cigarette cases, desk accessories, and jewelry.

Some of the highlights of art deco metalwork included Erik Magnusson's cubist coffee service, "The Lights and Shadows of Manhattan," Eliel Saarinen's spherical silver urn, and Peter Müller-Munk's exquisite designs, including his jazzy Normandie pitcher. The machine aesthetic inspired designs by Walter von Nessen, and the spun aluminum wares of Russel Wright.

The streamline phase of art deco was led by the industrial designer, a profession that developed to meet an urgent commercial need to attract new customers by repackaging a whole range of mass produced items, from railroad cars to pencil sharpeners, and including automobiles, office equipment, household appliances, radios and cameras. The leading industrial designers were Walter Dorwin Teague, Raymond Loewy, Henry Dreyfuss, Lurelle Guild, George Sakier, Egmont Arens, Joseph Sinel, and John Vassos. Gilbert Rohde, Kem Weber, and Russel Wright concentrated on mass produced furniture and household accessories, while Donald Deskey sold his numerous product designs from outlets across Europe. Less practical were the often visionary designs of the "P. T. Barnum of industrial design," Norman Bel Geddes.

In the end, streamlining, despite its enthusiastically promoted functionalism, was in effect a surface veneer – a repackaging in modernistic shell of the unwieldy and frequently unaltered machine parts beneath. The style's main function was to attract new customers by means of its persuasive allusions to efficiency, speed, modernism, and high style. The broader implication of streamlining included an optimistic desire to move forward – decisively, quickly and with little friction – leaving behind forever the chaotic social realities of the depression years.

Harold van Doren and J.G. Rideout
Radio, 1930-33, plastic, metal, and glass
Made by Air-King Products Company
Purchased with Funds donated by The Walter Foundation
The Brooklyn Museum, Brooklyn, NY

Noritake Art Deco Porcelain
Susy Skier (top)
Dutch Sunrise Landscape (bottom)
Photo: Joshua Schreier

Frederick Carder, Steuben Glass Works
Green Jade Prong Vase, ca. mid-1920s
The Rockwell Museum, Corning, NY

95

Frederick Carder, Steuben Glass Works
"Paperweight" Colognes, ca. late 1920s
The Rockwell Museum, Corning, NY

95

Pocket Watch, Gorham Company
ca. 1935, silver and enamel
Gift of Furman Hebb
Virginia Museum of Fine Arts, Richmond, VA

Sidney Waugh, Steuben Glass Works
Gazelle Bowl, 1935, colorless glass
Steuben Glass

Frederick Carder, Steuben Glass Works
Acid-etched Aurene Vase, 1927
The Rockwell Museum, Corning, NY

Frederick Carder, Steuben Glass Works
Acid-etched Vases, ca, 1925
The Rockwell Museum and the Corning Museum of Glass,
Corning, NY

OVERLEAF:
Tray, ca. 1935, chrome, painted glass, and wood
Gift of Sanford L. Smith & Associates
The Brooklyn Museum, Brooklyn, NY

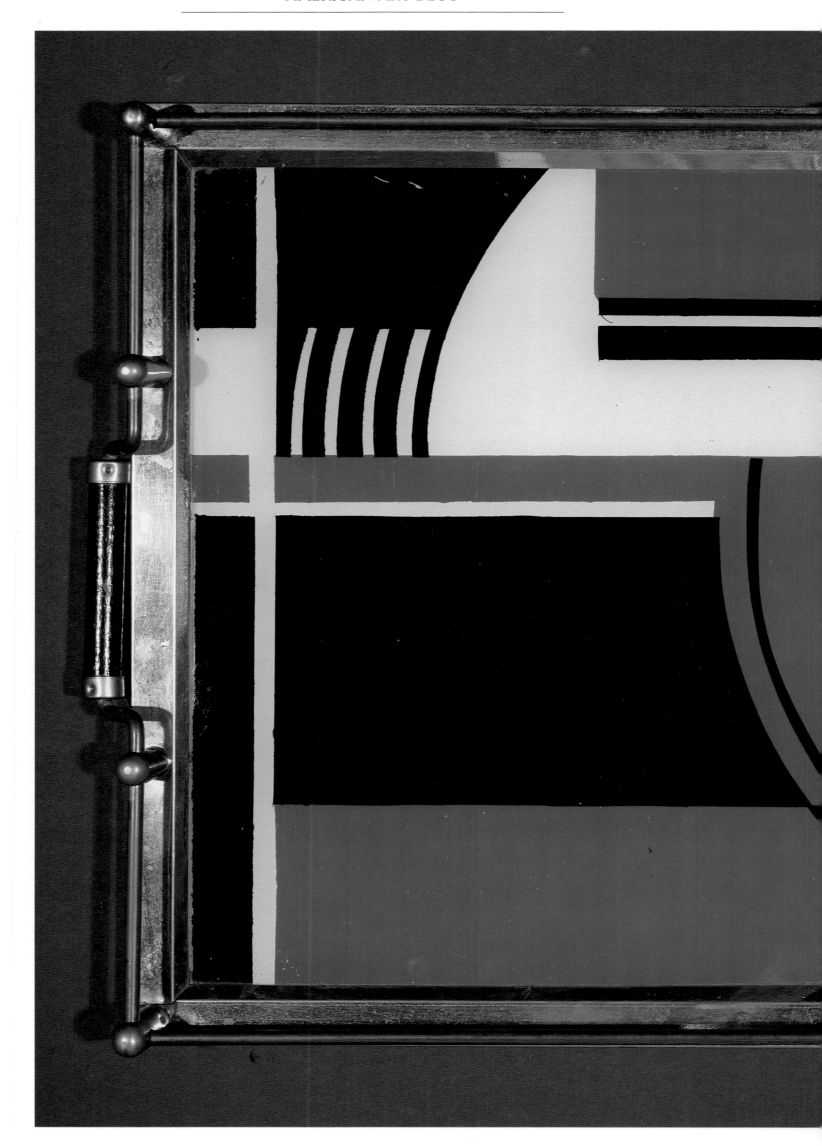

LEFT:
Attributed to **Kem Weber**
Coffee and Tea Service, ca. 1935-40
silver, ivory, and bakelite
The Mitchell Wolfson, Jr. Collection, courtesy
The Wolfsonian Foundation, Miami, FL

Eliel Saarinen
Urn and tray, 1934, silver
Cranbrook Academy of Art/Museum
Photograph courtesy of The Detroit Institute of Arts

103

Harlequin ware (left column)
Fiesta ware (right column), mid-1930s
Photo: © Schecter Lee/ESTO. All rights reserved

RIGHT:
Norman Bel Geddes
"Soda King" syphon bottle, ca. 1935
chrome-plated and enamelled metal with rubber fittings
H. Randolph Lever Fund
The Brooklyn Museum, Brooklyn, New York

Walter Dorwin Teague for Steuben Glass Works
Vase, 1932, colorless glass
Gift of Steuben Glass
The Corning Museum of Glass, Corning, NY

Walter Dorwin Teague
Camera and box, n.d.
Made by Eastman Kodak Company
H. Randolph Lever Fund
The Brooklyn Museum, Brooklyn, NY

Frederick Carder, Steuben Glass Works
Colorless luminors, ca. 1929
The Rockwell Museum, Corning, NY

Lurelle Guild
Vacuum cleaner, 1937
Made by Electrolux Corp.
The Brooklyn Museum, Brooklyn, NY

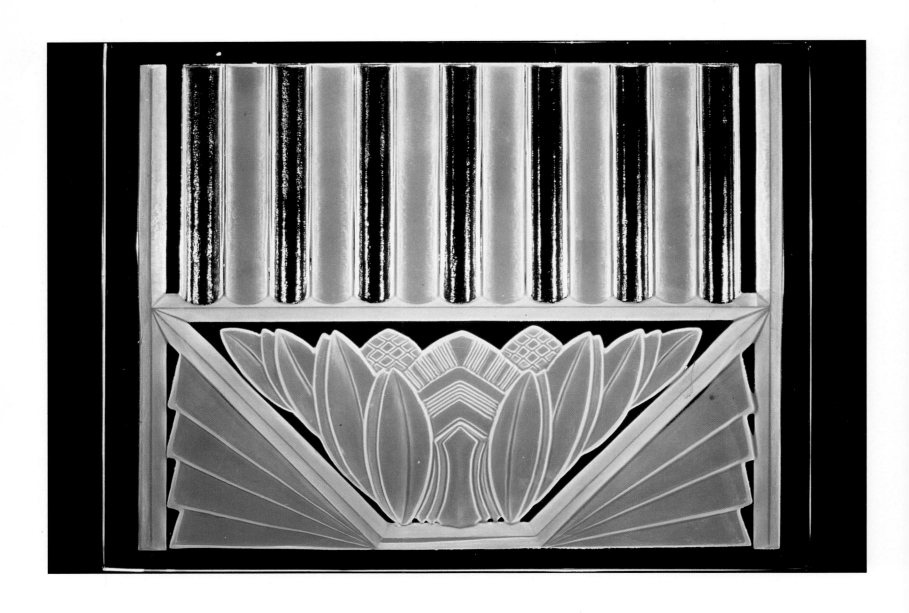

Paul Gardner
Lighting panel from Empire State Building
1931, crystal glass
The Corning Museum of Glass, Corning, NY

Wineglass, "#3011 line"
1930s, purple and colorless; mold-blown, pressed
Gift of Long Island Depression Glass Society
Cambridge Glass Co., Cambridge, OH

"Apple Blossom" wineglass
1932-40, colorless and pale blue glass
Made by Cambridge Glass Company, Cambridge, OH
The Corning Museum of Glass, Corning, NY

Salver, "American Sweetheart"
1930-1936, red glass, machine-pressed
Gift of Long Island Depression Glass Society
MacBeth-Evans Glass Co., Charleroi, PA

Bowl, "Everglade"
1930s, pale blue; pressed
Gift of the Long Island Depression Glass Society
Cambridge Glass Company, Cambridge, OH

INDEX

Acknowledgments
The author and publisher would like to thank the following people who helped in the preparation of this book: Don Longabucco, the designer; Susan Bernstein, the editor; and Liz Montgomery, the picture researcher.

Photo Credits
Art Institute of Chicago, 11
Auburn Cord Dusenberg Museum, 13
Bildarchiv d. Ost. Nationalbibliothek, 8
British Architectural Library, 6
Brompton Picture Library, 14
Chicago Historical Society, 12 (left)
The Corning Museum of Glass, 1, 3-4
Nembhard Culin, 12 (right)
ESTO Photographics: © Peter Mauss, 2; © Ezra Stoller, 16, 17
Everson Museum of Art, © Courtney Frisse, 9 (top)
© Balthazar Korab Ltd., 15 (bottom)
Minnesota Historical Society, 10
MOMA/Film Stills Archive, 9 (bottom)
Julius Shulman, 15 (top)
Werner Forman Archive, 7